Ukulele *from the* Beginning

Pop Songs
The Red Book

CHESTER MUSIC

Published by
Chester Music

Exclusive Distributors:
Hal Leonard
7777 West Bluemound Road
Milwaukee, WI 53213
Email: info@halleonard.com

Hal Leonard Europe Limited
42 Wigmore Street
Marylebone, London, W1U 2RY
Email: info@halleonardeurope.com

Hal Leonard Australia Pty. Ltd.
4 Lentara Court
Cheltenham, Victoria, 3192 Australia
Email: info@halleonard.com.au

Order No. CH81147
ISBN 978-1-78305-121-2
This book © Copyright 2013 Chester Music.
All rights reserved. International copyright secured.

Book content and layout by Camden Music.
Compiled by Christopher Hussey.
Edited by Toby Knowles.

Printed in the EU.

www.halleonard.com

About the series

This songbook uses the chords and picking patterns taught in *Ukulele from the Beginning Book 2*. As well as making this an ideal companion book for anyone working through the *Ukulele from the Beginning* course, *Pop Songs: The Red Book* is also an enjoyable standalone song collection for anyone learning to play the ukulele. Even an absolute beginner will find this collection of new and classic pop songs very accessible and easy to follow.

Contents

About this book

Here's a great selection of pop songs to add to your repertoire! They use only what you have learnt in *Ukulele From The Beginning Books 1* and *2*, featuring most of the chords that you know by the end of *Book 2*, as well as the strumming and fingerpicking patterns you have been taught.

Below are the fingerpicking patterns that you'll need for songs in this book, and opposite is a library of all the chords used.

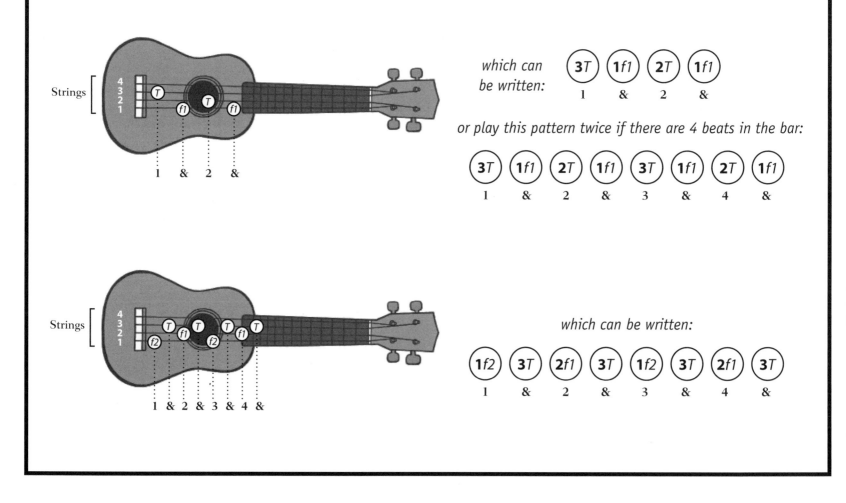

Chord Library

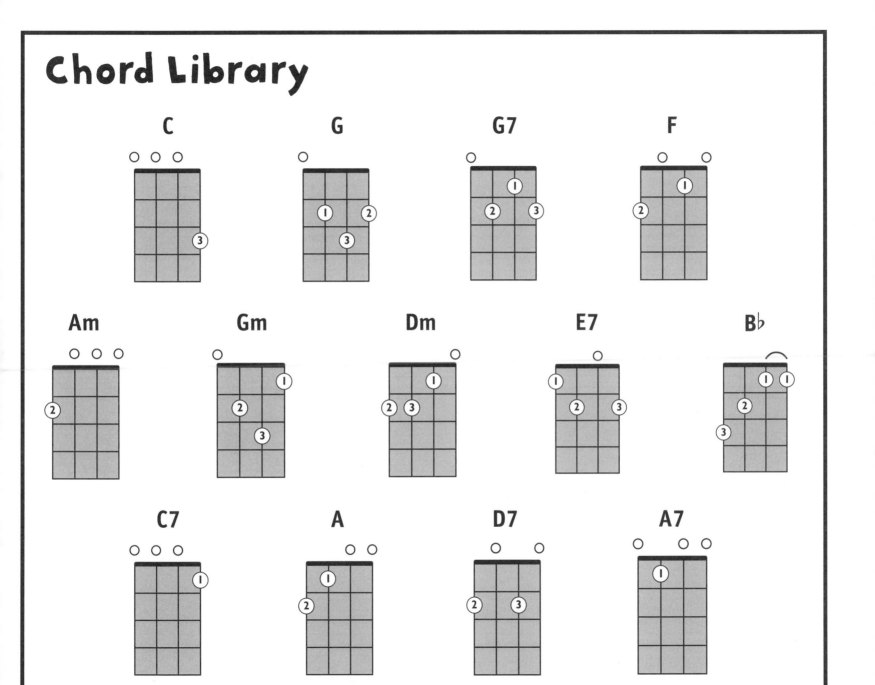

Hey Jude

Words & Music by John Lennon & Paul McCartney

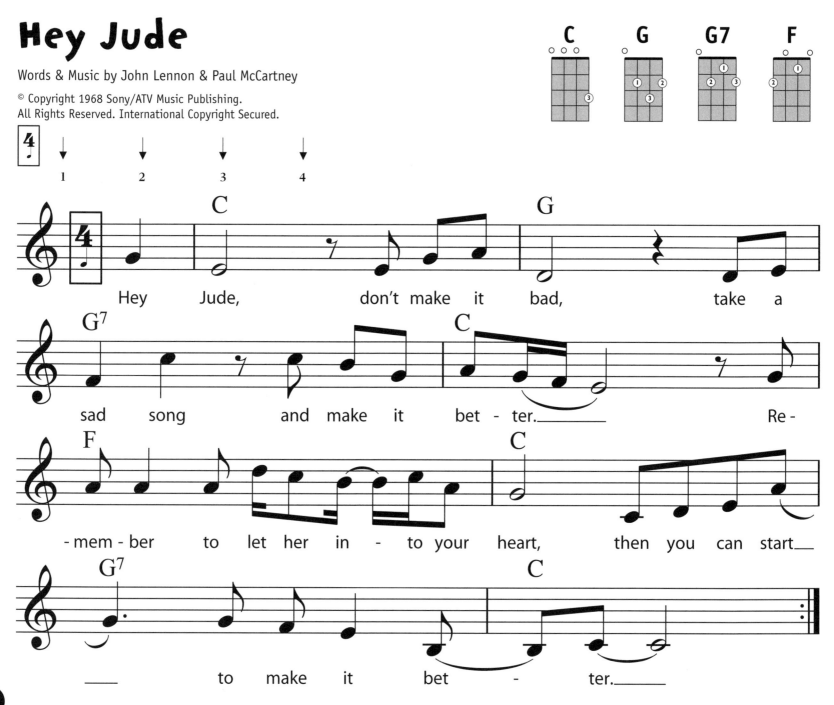

Candy

Words & Music by Robbie Williams, Gary Barlow & Terje Olsen

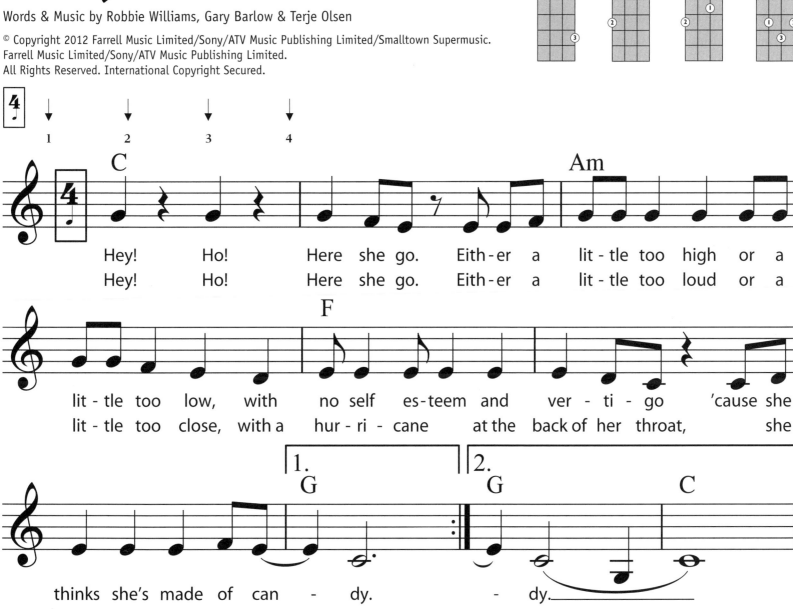

Hey! Ho! Here she go. Eith-er a lit-tle too high or a
Hey! Ho! Here she go. Eith-er a lit-tle too loud or a

lit-tle too low, with no self es-teem and ver-ti-go 'cause she
lit-tle too close, with a hur-ri-cane at the back of her throat, she

thinks she's made of can - dy.
thinks she's made of can -

- dy.

Catch My Breath

Words & Music by Kelly Clarkson, Jason Halbert & Eric Olson

Catch - ing my breath, let - ting it go, turn - ing my cheek for the sake of the show. Now that you know, this is my life,_____ I won't be

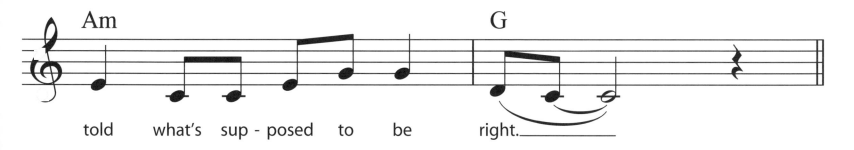

told   what's   sup - posed   to   be   right._____

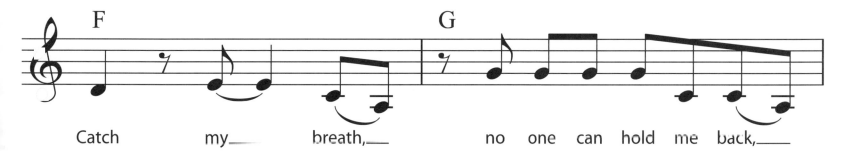

Catch   my___   breath,___   no   one   can   hold   me   back,___

I   ain't   got   time   for   that.___   Catch   my___   breath,___

won't   let 'em   get   me   down;___   it's   all   so   sim - ple   now.___

Someone Like You

Words & Music by Adele Adkins & Daniel Wilson

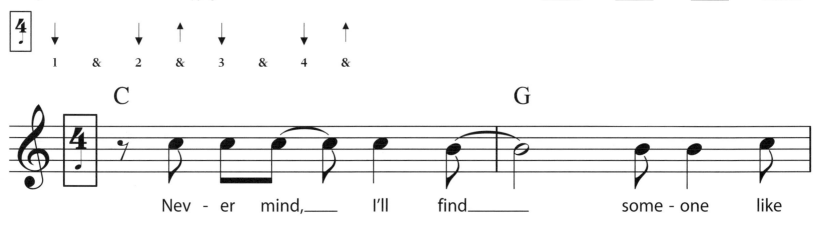

Nev - er mind,____ I'll find____ some - one like

you._____ I wish noth - ing____ but the

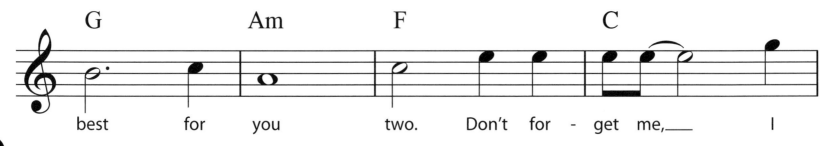

best for you two. Don't for - get me,____ I

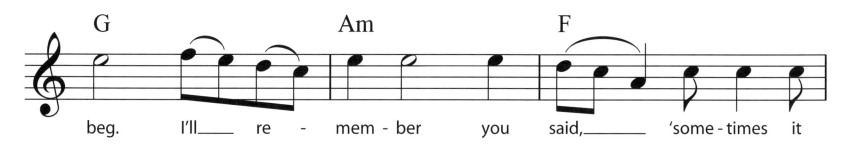

beg.   I'll___ re - mem - ber   you   said,_____ 'some - times   it

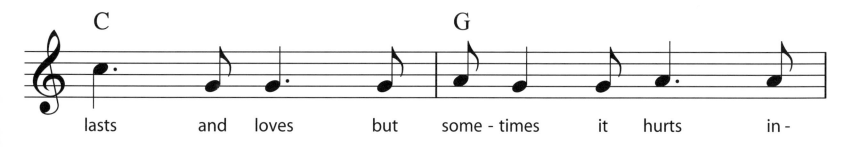

lasts   and   loves   but   some - times   it   hurts   in -

- stead._____   Some - times   it   lasts   and   loves   but

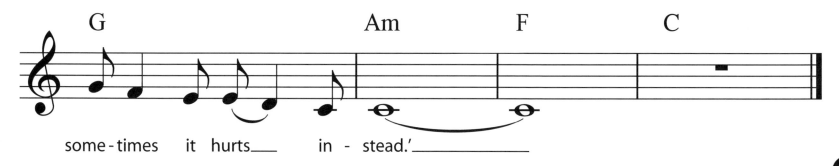

some - times   it   hurts___   in - stead.'_____

11

Ho Hey

Words & Music Jeremy Fraites & Wesley Schultz

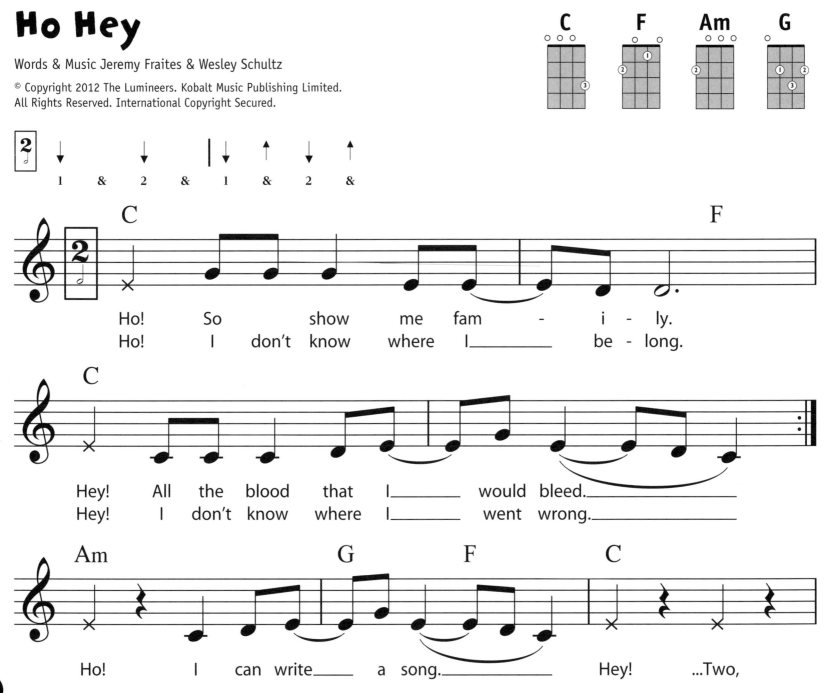

Ho!   So   show   me   fam   -   i - ly.
Ho!   I   don't   know   where   I_____   be - long.

Hey!   All   the   blood   that   I_____   would   bleed._____
Hey!   I   don't   know   where   I_____   went   wrong._____

Ho!   I   can   write_____   a   song._____   Hey!   ...Two,

Fight For This Love

Words & Music by Steve Kipner, Wayne Wilkins & Andre Merritt

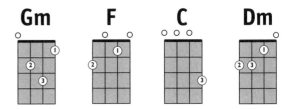

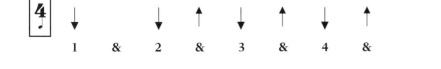

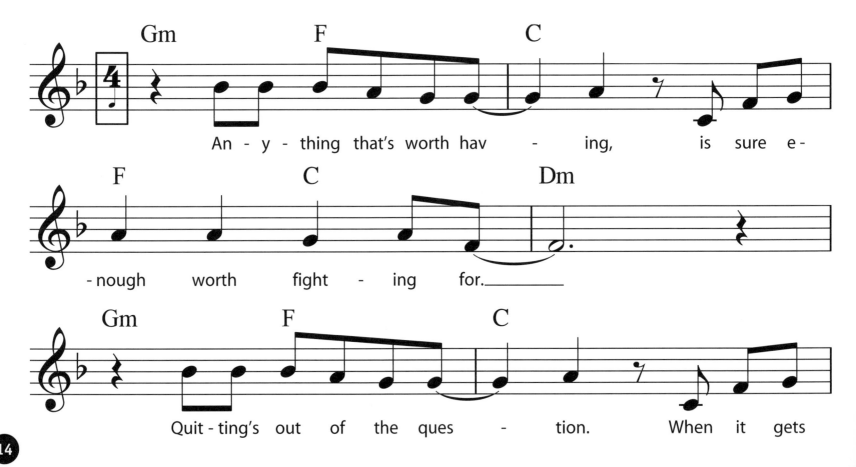

An - y - thing that's worth hav - ing, is sure e - nough worth fight - ing for.___

Quit - ting's out of the ques - tion. When it gets

14

Hallelujah

Words & Music by Leonard Cohen

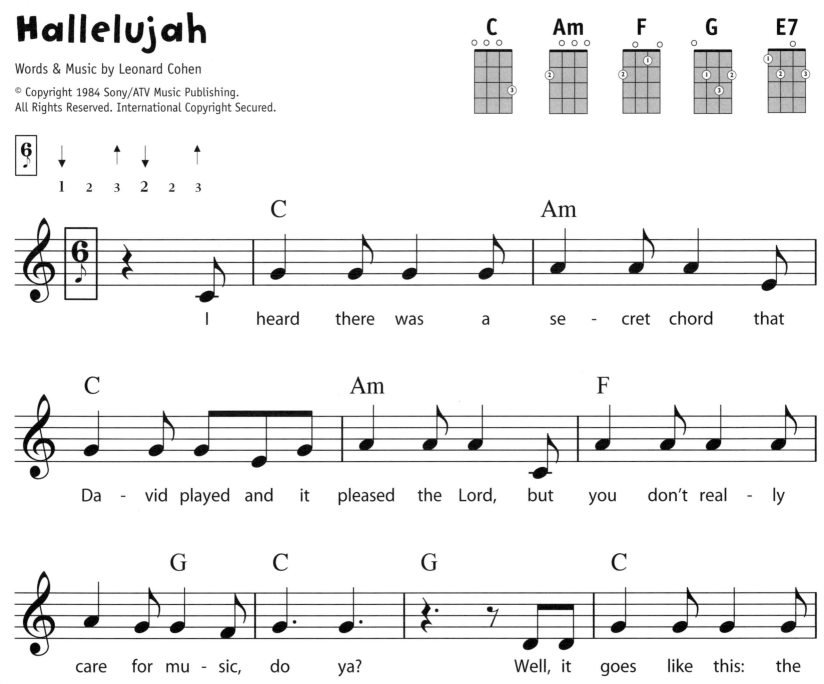

I heard there was a se - cret chord that

Da - vid played and it pleased the Lord, but you don't real - ly

care for mu - sic, do ya? Well, it goes like this: the

fourth, the fifth, the mi - nor fall and the ma - jor lift, the baf - fled king com -

-pos - ing 'Hal - le - lu - jah.'___ Hal - le - lu - jah,

hal - le - lu - jah, hal - le - lu - jah,

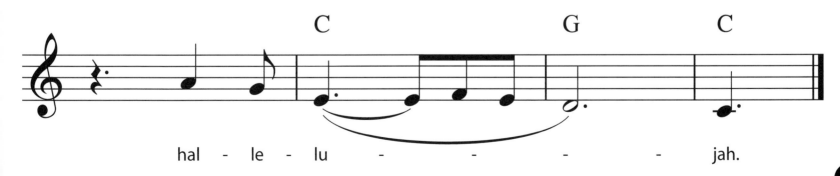

hal - le - lu - - - - jah.

Imagine

Words & Music by John Lennon

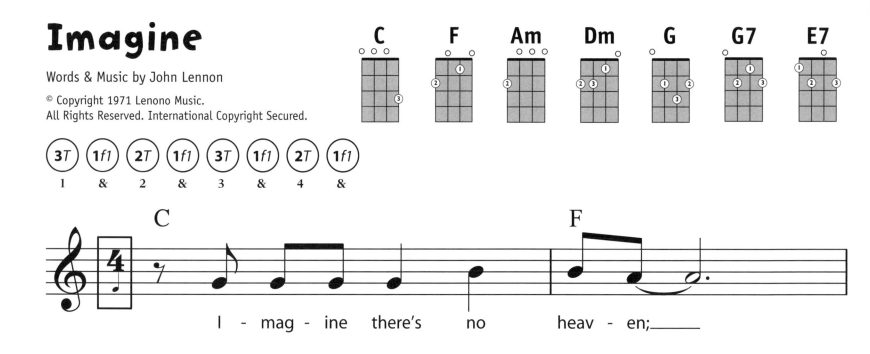

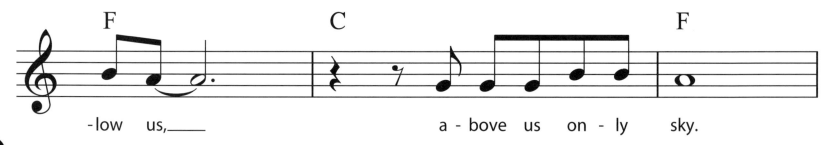

Lean On Me

Words & Music by Bill Withers

C   F   G7

C **F**

Lean on me_____ when you're not strong,_____ and I'll be your friend,

C **G⁷** **C**

_____ I'll help you car - ry on;_____ for, it won't be long_____

F **C** **G⁷** **C**

_____ 'til I'm gon-na need_____ some-bod-y to lean_____ on._____

What Makes You Beautiful

Words & Music by Savan Kotecha, Carl Falk & Rami Yacoub

Ba - by you light up__ my world like__ no - bod - y else. The way that

you flip__ your hair gets__ me o - ver - whelmed. But when you

smile at__ the ground, it__ ain't hard to tell: you don't__

know,_____ you don't know you're beau - ti - ful.__

Take A Bow

Words & Music by Mikkel Eriksen, Tor Erik Hermansen &
Shaffer Smith

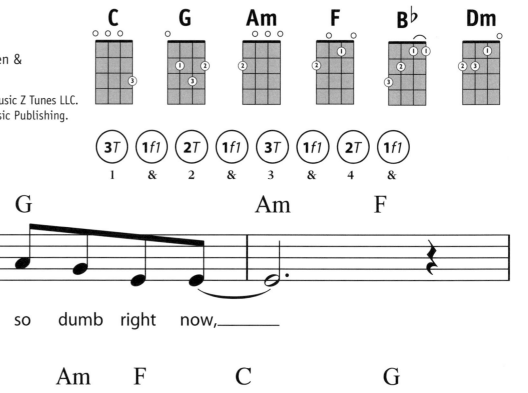

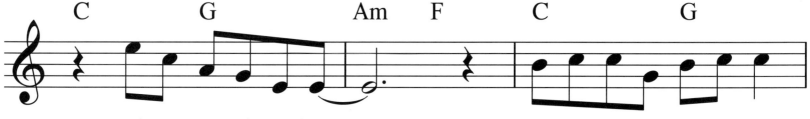

You look so dumb right now,_____

stand - ing out-side my house,___ try - ing to a - pol - o - gise,

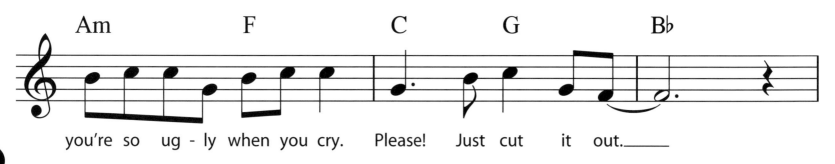

you're so ug - ly when you cry. Please! Just cut it out.____

Rule The World

Words & Music by Mark Owen, Gary Barlow, Jason Orange &
Howard Donald

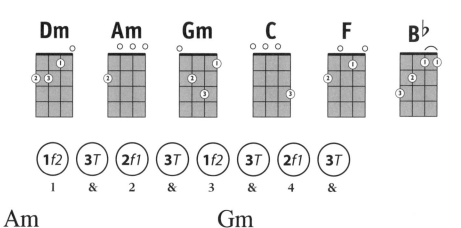

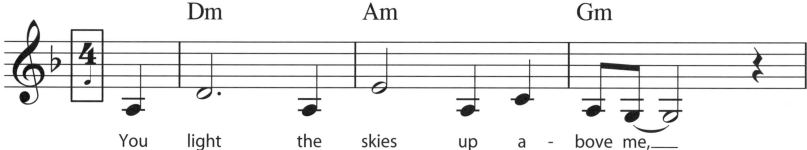

You light the skies up a - bove me, a star so bright you

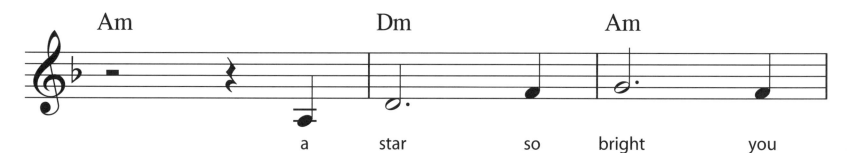

blind me,___ yeah,___ yeah. Don't close your

Somewhere Only We Know

Words & Music by Tim Rice-Oxley, Tom Chaplin & Richard Hughes

26

Grenade

Words & Music by Phillip Lawrence, Peter Hernandez,
Christopher Brown, Ari Levine, Claude Kelly & Andrew Wyatt

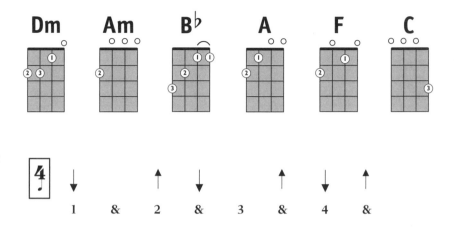

-nade for ya, throw my hand on a blade for ya, I'd jump in front of a train for ya; You know I'd do an-y-thing for ya. Oh,___ oh, I would go through all of this pain,___ take a bul-let straight through my brain.___ Yes, I would die for you ba - by, but you won't do the same.

Bridge Over Troubled Water

Words & Music by Paul Simon

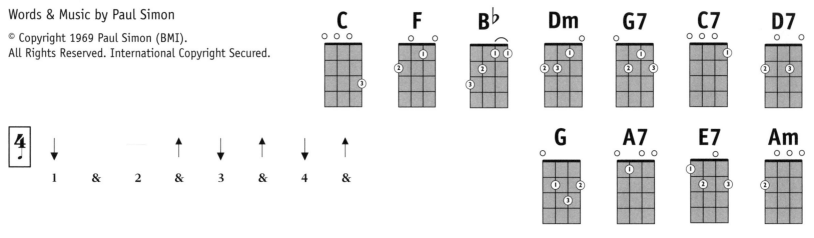

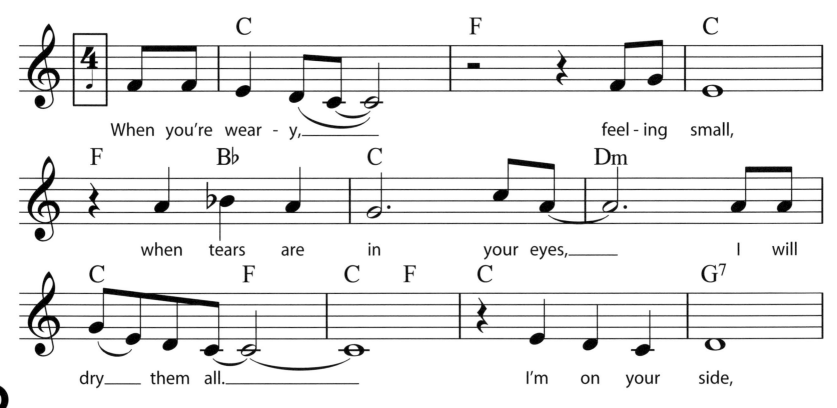

When you're wear - y,_____ feel - ing small,

when tears are in your eyes,_____ I will

dry____ them all._____ I'm on your side,

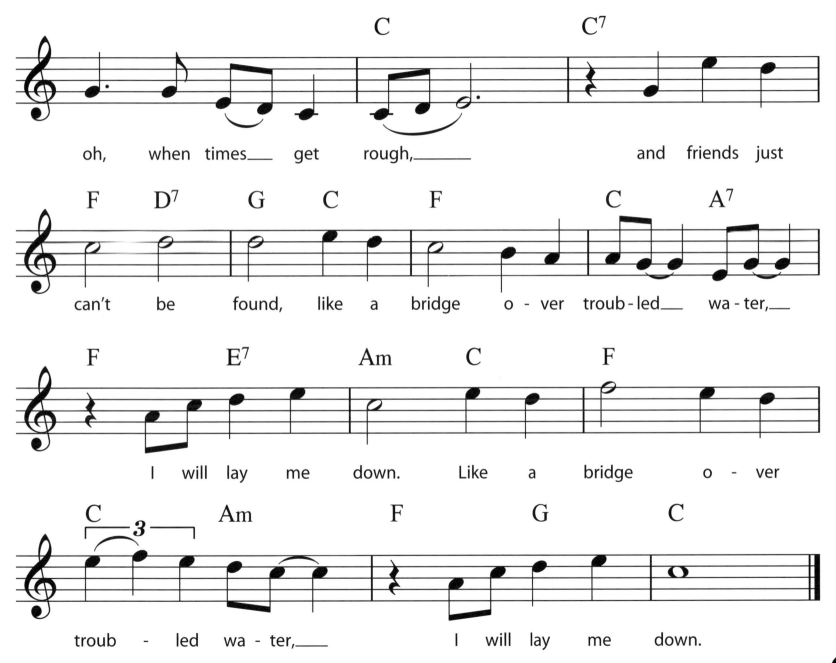

Everytime

Words & Music by Britney Spears & Annette Stamatelatos

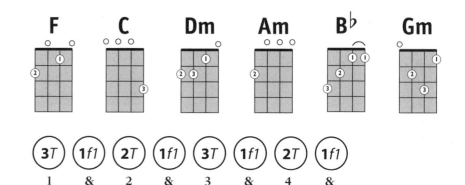

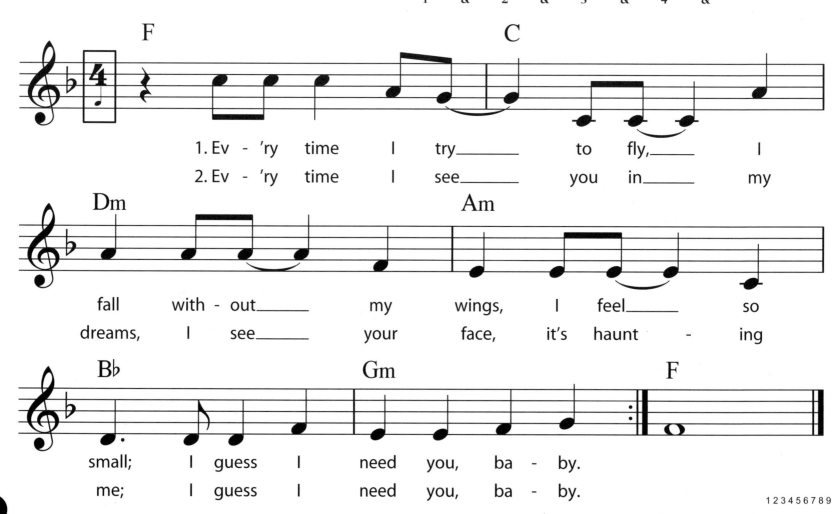

1. Ev - 'ry time I try_____ to fly,_____ I

2. Ev - 'ry time I see_____ you in_____ my

fall with - out_____ my wings, I feel_____ so

dreams, I see_____ your face, it's haunt - ing

small; I guess I need you, ba - by.

me; I guess I need you, ba - by.

123456789